Donna—

Enjoyed meeting
you, listening to
your stories. You're
a beautiful
spirit.

Love
Angie

Shadows of Fame, Volume I

Angie Carmen Thomas

VANTAGE PRESS
New York

FIRST EDITION

Published by Vantage Press, Inc.
516 West 34th Street, New York, New York 10001

Manufactured in the United States of America
ISBN: 0-533-12217-1

Library of Congress Catalog Card No.: 96-90933

0 9 8 7 6 5 4 3 2 1

To the beautiful Arianne Nicole Ramos, my niece, who appreciates the importance of books.

An artist, if he is truly an artist,
wants to do the will of God
and he must.

—Marvin Gaye

Contents

Preface

. . . a journey through the artistry of success
inspired me to share the
discoveries of my muses' artistry
which is reflected and revealed
through my poetry, their shadows. . . .

Acknowledgments

A very special thank you: Jean Auel, for sharing the experience you encountered when developing the *Clan of the Cave Bear,* an idea that played over within your mind, like a song, refusing to lose the struggle to survive; Bobby Joe Thomas, Jr. (my very special husband), for your love, your tremendous support, and your friendship; Else E. and Frank M. Simmons (Mom and Dad) for teaching me to search for the beauty that each person naturally possesses; Marina B. Ramos, my sister, for caring endlessly for me and always loving me; and Hildeguard Geisela Booth, for her unending belief in me.

Shirley Castonguay, thank you for encouraging me to fulfill my dreams; Louise Buttermore, for guiding my strengths; Joan Gallimore, for sharing your wisdom; Susie DuRocher, for supporting everything I try to accomplish; Robert Booth and James Ramos for filling my life with laughter, comedy, and fun; Rick and Linda Jenkins and Christopher Savage and your answering machine . . . for your genuine friendship; Rachel and Alan Taggart, Christopher and Richard Dowdy for photographic memories of our lasting friendship.

Thank you, Steve and Alice Edwards, for allowing me to absorb Mother Nature's inspiration at Moonwater Cabin. Thank you, Aunt Sandra Smith, for filling my life with fragrant flowers. Thank you Mike, Juanita, Candice and Dennisa Booth for the laughter and fun at family gatherings.

Special appreciation from my heart to Gary Herring, Debbie Mello, Jessica and Gary Herring, Jr., Jessica Graves, and Josh Mello. You guys are the best neighbors anyone could ever have. Deb, thanks for the ice tea! Gary, thanks for the spicy chicken wings! And all of you, thank you so much for allowing me to decorate at your picnics! Luv ya.

And most dear to me, Elizabeth Brown, my Home Interior Distributor, beautiful Betty . . . a precious friend and lovely woman who always makes me feel special. Thank you for decorating my life with beauty and elegance.

There are many more friends and family to thank for their love and inspiration during my lifetime, and each volume of *Shadows* will reflect those very special people.

Thank you, Lord, for this opportunity to share my poetry. You're an inspirational partner showering me with spiritual "ideas." I'm truly blessed that you lead me through this fantastic journey and may this volume be just the beginning.

In Memory of Gene Kelly

. . . who asserted his creativity by displaying an acceptable temperament
that effectively released his inner talent . . .
and for fearlessly pursuing the desires of his creative soul by dancing with its shadow . . .

Introduction

Discover a Shadow

Every artist proves himself worthy of that persistent
insistence
of the inner creativity alive in his soul;
whose craving to be revealed is done so by becoming a reality
through the multitude of forms available
within the universe.

The substance deep within succeeds
through recognition of doing the will of God.
The avenues leading to the destiny of an artist's soul
takes the power within to an intersection
of choices. . .

Choosing the next road towards success
seems dependent
upon a greater power . . .
the guiding source
towards acceptance.

Exploration of Inspiration

Exploring success began a journey into the world of famous
people by exploring the essence of artistry to discover the pur-
pose of creative survival. The power of creativity appears to be
awakened by the pursuit of dreams, free to be carried into reality
. . . through an internal gravity that invites intense desires into
the soul for quiet discovery, emerging with the natural purpose
of becoming successful.

Dreams that are now reality and have endured the exciting
demands of creativity have filled my soul with admiration, a

cherished treasure, inspiring me to respond to the powerful influence of famous people through the expression of poetry . . . and survive with the natural purpose of giving my muses a cherished treasure.

Taking this journey into *Shadows of Fame* will reveal the impact of artistry that touched the power within me. This power deep within my soul, led me to discover the unique treasures of many shadows that are released through creative artistry . . . and revealed through fame.

Shadows of Fame, Volume I

Shadow: Italian Strokes
Muse: Giorgio de Chirico, Painter

it is 1917 . . . a canvas
pure white like clouds after rain
is destined to be a creation. . .

an Italian artist begins to paint colorful
strokes of carefully chosen oils shaping history
merged with glimpses into time to come

figures of mythology appear,
the muses that rule artistry;
one mysteriously stands in the depths of a shadow

the meaning of the muses
takes the creative talent
which is within the soul

and brings it to life
through physical forms,
the essence behind fame . . .

living on a pure white canvas
entitled
"The Menacing Muses"

a painting examined
in 1996. . .

Shadow: Places
Muse: Thomas Moore, Author

The soul wants to be revealed, not understood.
—Thomas Moore

The creation of film becomes a physical form,
combining the efforts of talented souls
emerging as a final product of artistry
designed to capture an audience.

A portrayal of characters is a study . . . of life's survival
reenacting virtues which relate to an audience.
Each character strives to find the intended direction
through the support of one who maintains the story
with intentions to work together to finish the film.

Behind the characters,
editors relieve the footage of unnecessary images
to strengthen a film's message and bring it to life . . .
in places destined to magnify the creativity
of the characters who reveal the story.

Shadow: Invitation
Muse: Whoopi Goldberg, Actress

. . .I can still remember . . .
hearing the
softness in your voice
and seeing the sparkle in your
eyes . . .

as you invited all people to pursue their talents
and strive to connect
with those who are already deep
into pursuing
their dreams . . .

with the intention of learning
from one another
while being inspired
to travel those paths
meant for success

and for the absorption of
knowledge
that lies
on the journey
towards our destiny . . .

Shadow: Flight of Approval
Muse: Steven Spielberg, Director

Reaching the boundary . . .
physical senses become attentive,
discussing the alternatives, they chose to soar into creativity
and float within the sphere of ideas . . .
the passage to unknown limitations.

Adjusting with comfort, exposed to spontaneity,
the senses begin their investigation of a natural environment.
The eyes stare into the imagination capturing the beginning of a
thought . . .
hands touch the mental images within the mind, shaping the process of
development.
The nose breathes life into attained knowledge, an aroma of successful
direction . . .

entices hunger to taste the purpose of comprehension,
attracting vibrations of precision,
developing the sound of experiences already encountered,
influencing the soul to seek agreement among the physical senses
requesting a decision based on the evidence discovered within this
portion of the creative journey.

The heart becomes aware of its role as mediator
to intervene before submission of validity occurs,
observing the idea created
within the sphere of spontaneity,
applying rules of reason to justify application.

The soul takes control of the heart and of the mind
deciding that the passage to unknown limitations
served its ultimate purpose. . .
Thoughts based on sincerity evolve into a determined desire
to translate a story which survives
by passionately touching those who cannot soar into creativity. . .

Shadow: Confrontation
Muse: Sidney Poitier, Actor

each of us have a gift deep within our soul
that wants to be confronted and released
—Angie Thomas

. . .in stillness, the soul waits,
listening for auditory tremors . . .
contemplating the origins
from which sounds of dreams will come.

The soul asks itself how it will explain
the shadow of obscurity to its creator,
and in silence, the soul's breath touches the hidden gem of its layers
reaching to free its beauty from years of life's challenges.

The soul stares longingly at its innocence
with adoration and wonder . . .
How did it survive the crimes of life
and still remain untouched, shining in the darkness.

Many people reach deep within themselves
to reveal the gem of their soul's passion,
feeling that burning desire to understand
and conquer . . . a mystery called the creative process.

Shadow: Courageous Preservation
Muses: Roy Uwe Ludwig Horn . . . Siegfried Fischbacher
Siegfried and Roy, Entertainers

Germany, the point of origin left behind
for the pursuit of discovery.
Two teenagers travel alone
finding dreams in another land
searching for a mission in life.

Preserving a distinguished form of domestication,
preventing the destruction of beauty,
allowing courage and strength
to exist within a powerful, gentle durability,
protecting the innocence and magnificence of white lions and tigers. . .

Creating harmony around you
appears to radiate from your
deep understanding of extinction,
and the immense gratification that evolves
from the love living within your souls.

. . .and it is those qualities
you possess that overflow with proof
that existence of logic living in the mind
is freely given to the soul . . . giving the world a gift of purpose
which fulfills your mission.

Shadow: Sailing the Sea
Muse: Barbra Streisand, Singer

I adore the feelings that surface from within me
when your voice celebrates the substance of your soul
filling my soul with breath . . .
absorbing songs that touch
my heart.

You are ageless . . .
forever radiating innocence and beauty,
penetrating the atmosphere
with gentle drops of power
vibrating the sound barrier of strength

with emotions,
hypnotizing my feelings
with reflections from your eyes,
. . . a thousand thoughts
living in seas of blue . . .

Expanding the knowledge within my mind,
I reach the core of experiences
with courage and certainty,
enabling me to realize the beauty
which exists within you . . .

Shadow: A Great Man
Muse: Bill Cowher
Pittsburgh Steelers *Football Coach*

A great coach . . .
committed to the team, determination colors your eyes
witnessing skills of shades of black and gold
guided by your strength of positive reinforcement;
a performance of skill motivated by a dedication
found within you and challenged by a concept
which you have stirred within the team,
reminding them of what is . . . and is not important.

A great person . . .
guided by God, you find the purpose for football.
Divine knowledge lives within you;
fans witness the wisdom
that He accomplishes through you.
A mission to give your management style . . . freely,
to a group of golden men
who realize the meaning of success.

A great leader . . .
possessing physical bravery,
a jawbone of strength, eyes of ocean-deep devotion,
the stairway to your soul.
Your heart descends the stairs of sensitivity,
through the perfection of your thoughts;
orchestrating your words into a musical of sensitive feelings
that create effective relationships born from a deep desire

to be a great man . . .

Shadow: Exposure
Muse: Sinbad, Comedian

An earring . . .
sparkles on a stage;
a glittering elevation above eyes of fans.
Pants and shirts . . . loose and comfortable
reveals your style.

A microphone radiates a voice
penetrating the laughter below
causing the atmosphere to be
filled with your talent
for exposing reality.

Your artistry easily demands that
frustration be released from within,
causing your fans to smile,
laugh, and accept reality
for what it is . . .

By seeing it through the
eyes of a comedian.

Shadow: A Gift of Grace
Muse: Julia Roberts, Actress
Something to Talk About

Existing on the Davant Plantation,
bonded by experiences of disloyalty
surrendering the heart to social obligations,
required to behave respectably
barely surviving the duty expected to support tradition.

Silently conforming
to the sense of responsibility
by accepting secrets of disrespect,
forced to trade the chance of freedom
for loyalty.

One man allowed exaggerated pride to become significant
drowning in the past, disappointing the present, suffocating the future,
for the purpose of ensuring
that others maintain low expectations,
a gift deteriorating through generations.

Your inner conscience tingled . . . exploded within your heart
and a sense of what is right and proper
emerged through your actions,
helping those pieces of tradition that are right
take their places within today's society.

You chose to continue those traditions
that are still acceptable and thoughtful,
repairing the wrongs of the past
by breaking the silence of disloyalty,
shattering the hearts of those you love . . .

which led to the restoration of their souls.
Releasing the tension which caused suppression
allowed freedom to surface . . .
restoring self-respect
and the meaning of pride.

Taking the time necessary
to understand disappointment,
healed your heart and you realized
that maintaining low expectations
suffocates the very essence of soul, dreams.

You trusted the inner dreams of those who wanted the chance
to make them a reality . . . giving Hank and Caroline
the gift of grace
allowed them the freedom
to live their dreams, possessing the right to become a reality.

Through that gift, your own dreams became possible
as you boldly took that chance to be who you really are,
leaving the consequences in the hands of destiny.
A tradition of inner strength free to everyone
and that is something to talk about!

Shadow: Kalua and Cream
Muses: Richard Pryor and Gene Wilder, Actors

I ordered a Kalua and Cream,
using the skinny straw to slowly stir
the shades of black and white.
My thoughts soared to memories locked within.

I was sad, it had been a messy day, filled with hardships
and I needed a good laugh.
I finished my drink and drove to Video Update,
grabbed Stir Crazy *and rushed home, smiling.*

The essence of your creativity was absorbed instantly.
Just seeing your faces
lightened the day's load
and I was mesmerized by your abilities as a team. . .

Your wild and crazy antics satisfied my hunger
for uncontrollable laughter.

It is a privilege to watch your creativity
and I thank God for His wisdom,
ensuring that the two of you found one another on this Earth
to give the world the purest form of laughter.

Shadow: Shades of Enchantment
Muse: Roma Downey, Actress

Irish echoes . . . fill my spirit with comfort.
You are a beautiful soul
living within a crystal decanter
filled with shades of enchantment,
a shadow of an Angel . . .

Thought-provoking reality is
simply shown through your love;
each mission required
to entwine with the master plan
guiding those whose character sleeps in their souls.

The virtues you possess urges an awakening
. . . the ability to see . . .
that surrendering the past and present to a unknown future is absolute.
Belief is a requirement, no variables can sustain what one experiences
when radiance from your presence touches them,

absorbing doubts into a place forgotten,
and the tears stored within a lost soul
rush into the present to capture the beauty
of a dove . . . white, pure, free,
able to perform miraculous tasks,

assisting God in His quest
to penetrate all who have the
right to feel His compassion,
freely giving each person the courage to live
as intended.

Shadow: Aroma of Harmony
Muse: Bruce Lee, Martial Artist

Meditating to the sounds of windchimes
and the aroma of harmony . . .
quietly walking on the edges of my soul,
entering the invisible realm
of my identity.

Visiting memories incapable of extinction
surviving on the precise nature of your
discipline, enabling me to capture
a strength which no one can penetrate.

To gain self-control and maintain the knowledge
of my mind as my body soars high into visions of your character,
allows me to visit you and touch your face.
Closing my eyes, I smell the scent of your presence
and appreciate the art of meditation.

We talk, and I adore your smile, listening to your voice . . .
providing me with guidance, advising my soul
to always be obedient to my creativity,
. . . set it free. Never be afraid of uncertain pathways, answers are for
those who seek truth, never slow to react to that which is destined to
be . . .

Time to leave my companion of meditation . . .
I float back into the space of reality,
cherishing the moments,
remembering his beauty, his silence,
and know I can meet any challenge.

I begin to smile as I recall Bruce Lee's trademark,
the master of martial artistry . . .
The thumb against the nose,
informing his opponents
that they are now in serious trouble!

The aroma of harmony and sounds of windchimes
are interrupted by a knock at the door . . .
and I wonder, if I open it, will I see
a memory,
or be in the present . . . reality?

Shadow: Fragrant Embrace
Muse: Oprah Winfrey, Talk Show Host

An arrangement of fragrance . . . flowers
cut fresh, smiling.

Petals of integrity illuminate
the sparkle of your genuine identity.

Hope is revealed and embraced
in your presence.

Concern radiates from within
your soul, staring from understanding.

Compassionate and kind,
qualities of a woman who . . .

too has searched for hope
and embraced it

becoming the fragrance
of integrity.

Shadow: Natural Admiration
Muse: Demi Moore, Actress

Reaching a state of comfort
within a place where many are afraid of being
or know nothing about.

You have challenged yourself,
taking a journey into self-discovery
. . . one that is important . . . and necessary.

I admire your ability
to walk treacherous paths courageously,
shoving the boulders out of your way . . .

climbing mountains
that were natural,
. . . some built to hinder your passions.

Reaching the top of your artistry,
you smiled down upon those who understand
even smiling at those who didn't.

No one could have ever stopped you in the quest
to be uninhibited,
maintaining self-respect . . .

freeing the chains of fear,
allowing you to reach the state of admiration,
releasing the wonders of your soul.

You are a woman who nourishes your life with resilience,
growing from the knowledge that your spirit's possessions
are alive . . . and beautiful.

Shadow: Scottish Symphony
Muse: Mel Gibson, Actor

An old phonograph stares out the window,
watching the light of day disappear . . .
Beethoven's sonata "Für Elise," dances with the moonlight's breeze,
enabling me to indulge in a peaceful solitude
and contemplate the immense meaning of Braveheart.

Lighting plaid-painted candles, hundreds accumulated over the years,
I feed my meditation with flames of vanilla and magnolia,
and think about that man . . .
reliving the serene earthquake that shook me within, compassionately,
resulting in an eternal adoration for William Wallace.

He imbibed me
as he transformed from a human
into a symbol
representing the core essence
of admirable determination.

His Scottish phonology was remarkably innocent,
a simple and powerful message of unending encouragement
capturing the thoughts of men who wanted to believe,
idolizing the natural beauty of femininity
that all women crave.

William Wallace, I adore you for the manner in which you love
and live . . . intensely,
with a passionate perception,
void of any confusion
for the meaning of freedom.

Shadow: Thrilling
Muse: Sharon Stone, Actress

A roller coaster ride,
a scary movie
or perhaps the characteristics
of a stone . . .
beautiful, polished, radiant,

silently lying on the beach
staring into the sun
. . . a passage to sensuality.
Brass instruments
dance in a nearby jazz bar.

Smoke flows from her mouth,
her cigarette excited to be kissed by her lips
. . . arousing the feelings of the waves
thrashing the sand,
trying to touch her . . .

She is engulfed in this space
of pure desire,
her erotic eyes close and
blonde strands of hair
dry in the intensity of the heat.

She seduces the atmosphere and it melts.
She smiles erotically, lying on the beach,
like a stone, knowing the many characters
portrayed in her career
. . . are thrilling.

Shadow: Intimacy of Dreams
Muse: Eugenio Zanetti, Director
. . . inspired by the words "follow your dream"

One's dreams are surrounded by the
palisade of one's desire,
creating a refuge protecting
against the infections of
interference.

Crystallized stones form
the imprints of steps
taken on the mortal
investigation
of one's images.

to witness each declaration
saturated in affection
as each destination
is left behind for
the future demands of one's dreams.

Closely examining the accuracy
of each alien woven
within the space of truth
reveals which medium
to pursue.

ensuring the essential growth
of one's dreams, which must
be destined to live,
causing the palisade
to disappear.

until the next desire sparks
the intimacy of another dream . . .

Shadow: The Kidnaping
Muse: Jerry Lewis, Actor

You have always been in my life,
causing hysteria to kidnap me
carrying me into a world of laughter,
experiencing your portrayal of humorous characters.

The empty boardroom scene in The Errand Boy
is my favorite in the history of movie-making.
Your desire to experience importance
by pretending to be the top executive
exerting your power in the large cushioned chair,

smoking an unlit cigar
demanding invisible employees
listen to a speech
performed through musical instruments.

Your mouth forms the words,
but I hear a musical interpretation
of power without words,
which could be the essence of power.

Shadow: A Desert Nourished

Your dedication to MDA is itself a quality of who you are,
passionate about life's physical struggles,
forever carrying the strength of hope.

The desert was filled with musicians orchestrated by you,
and the sounds touched me . . . deeply.
It was playful, comical yet at the same time,
your thoughts were serious . . .

The innocence of children
must be preserved
to ensure their ability
to remain healthy and continue to grow.

The intensity of that scene
was created by your existence,
filling a barren desert with a musical prayer
. . . for a cure.

Shadow: Crimson Flames
Muse: Lucille Ball, Actress

Looking upward into a golden kingdom in the sky
I imagine the flight of angels
that surround your being
. . . happy to be in your presence . . .

Remembering the talented beauty in I Love Lucy
stirs the memories of laughter
that overwhelmed me,
warming my heart like flames of crimson, burning softly.

The fiery smile and funny faces you share
gives me contentment
. . . as I am absorbed
inside the reruns of another era,

honored by the presence of your brilliance,
and your natural abilities as an actress
which were incredibly hilarious,
filling my days with appreciation.

I admire your beauty,
your courage,
and will adore you, always . . .
feeling the warmth of crimson flames.

Shadow: Vacancy Filled
Muse: John Grisham, Author

Piercing eyes stare at me
from a book cover,
powerful, intriguing
. . . gentle.

Your writing talents are appreciated
and many of your followers
anxiously wait for another story
to be created.

Reading the thoughts that only you could have
allow the imagination to survive within your life experiences
and enjoy the tremendous ability you have
to bring those stories to life,

filling a vacant page
with images of your creativity
and style . . .
as the ink dries permanently, solidifying your artistry.

I recall your advice to aspiring writers,
"An author must succeed, fail, suffer, and
experience heartache
before he has anything to write about."

You have become very important,
an inspiration to my dream
of reaching the level of adoration
required for an immense following . . .

Shadow: Lavender Mist
Muse: Della Reese, Actress

. . . the very powerful and fresh scent
of lavender reminds me of
an aroma that a mighty
personality would possess.

Sprinkles of violet showers linger . . .
engraving your beauty
in the wings
of my heart . . .

challenging the depths
of lost dreams
to once again, surface
from my soul.

Running in fields of lavender
I crave the embrace
of your affection
and enjoy the splendor of freedom that

takes my breath away,
as my dreams
follow you
with new meaning,

baptized in the moisture of
a lavender mist,
feeling that I can someday
meet my dreams in reality.

Shadow: Soul of Saturn
Muse: Kay Redfield Jamison, Author

. . . the wonder of planets
lives beyond my touch
sleeping in the vastness
of space and time.

For those whose imagination is limitless,
a sense of beauty and security
is found within
both planet and person.

Cruising the altitude,
I am surrounded by planetary luminance
that dazzles my spirit
allowing serenity to fill my senses.

The universe is a treasure chest,
filled with sparkling old and new
pieces of jewelry
placed here somewhere . . . in time.

The circular embrace of golden glittering bracelets
guards the intensity of Saturn's Soul,
what lies beyond? within?
are questions that I already know the answers to.

I chose to leave Saturn behind,
soaring further into space.
Hearing the laughter of angels,
I want to glimpse their beauty,

and I have, many times on planet Earth.
They exist in many forms, as you do,
writing, sharing, helping people to grasp depression
and leave behind

the intensity of Saturn's Soul . . .
to soar towards a life of authenticity.

Shadow: Original Embraces
Muse: Patrick Robinson, Fashion Designer

Weaving ideas within the mind,
an excited glow appears in your eyes
as you process the visualizations
of your thoughts,

skillfully planning
an artistry of shapes, colors, and patterns
to ensure vibrancy
and adoration.

Assembling pieces of your imagination
with textures and designs
creating individuality
and . . . essence,

touching the shapes of completion, you feel its heartbeat
smiling as you watch many
adorn themselves with your ideas
by embracing their surroundings.

Shadow: Luxurious Simplicity
Muse: Fran Drescher, Actress

I painted a vision which entranced me,
taking me into the passages
of simplicity
to visit a beautiful woman with dark hair . . .

capturing her silhouette as she
lights silver and white candles.
I appreciate the shadows of those tiny fires
because they represent intense passion for ambiance.

I smell the peacefulness of the flowers
and in the midst of this abundant gathering
the beautiful woman with dark hair
falls asleep in her favorite chaise lounge,

snuggling in the cozy atmosphere of her garden,
soaking the warmth of the sun's last smile of the day
recalling the pathways walked throughout her life,
she begins to dream.

The radiance of her eyes as they open,
confide that she is content in this paradise
able to believe that the moon's glow is now a brilliant diamond,
images she would never sacrifice.

The beautiful woman with the dark hair
snuggles in the warmth by the flame of Monet.
Smelling the scent of jasmine entices her to rekindle memories
possessing the knowledge that comfort is simply luxurious.

Shadow: Dolphin Dive
Muse: Ellen DeGeneres, Actress

. . .

I am filled with jealousy . . .
you own a book store and I don't!
You are a blonde, me, just a brunette.
You are a phenomenal comedian, I guess I can be funny
and dye my hair blonde, and open a book store!
I'm glad that is solved!

. . .

The book you wrote filled my reading time with laughter,
giggles and many smiles.
Each chapter was filled with your ability
to create a continuous flow of thoughts gone overboard . . .

submerging in a world admired, discovering friendship at sea
smiling at happy, genuine faces of dolphins,
that capture you
within a sense of strength and security . . .

relying on the dolphins, another species
to guide your journey
through the world beneath land
and all its magnificent beauty.

You dive with your new friends
forming a loyal bond at sea,
drenched in the wonder
of your life in comedy.

I am captured by the genuine
sense of strength and security I feel
when I contemplate joining the dolphins
to experience the wonder of your soul.

Shadow: Planet Tap
Muse: Savion Glover, Choreographer

Somewhere within your quest
at a wonderful young age
you found yourself tapping
on a Broadway stage.

Dancing into space . . .
creating a unique beat
for a musical that
celebrates funk.

It seems that your imagination
wanders freely
within a sensitive style
that beats to a rhythm of your immense talent.

Strong and overwhelming techniques
excite audiences
who have the honor
of experiencing your creations.

Planets embrace your spirit,
a musical harmony sparkles like stars;
the soft, glistening reflections in your eyes
reveals future rhythms

of the universe,
which ultimately thrive with age
allowing your talents
to find its place on a Broadway stage.

Shadow: Genuine Pearl
Muse: Rosie O'Donnell, Talk Show Host

One incredible talk show every single day,
smiling and laughing, there is no better way

than joining you, your guests and staff
for a unique hour of variety, and a bouquet of laughs

that you create with ease,
relentlessly natural, whether you're serious or a tease.

You possess tremendous abilities as a host
loving sincerity I admire the most.

You are beautiful and smart
and I know that you will always play the part

that is genuine, lovable and kind . . .
like a pearl in an oyster, a rare treasure to find.

"Luv ya, call me."

Shadow: Shells of Silver
Muse: Lavine Hudson, Singer

"A Little Sensitivity"
<u>*In the House*</u>

Words chimed in harmony,
upbeat and happy.
Your smile, genuine and natural
a song sung from within your soul.

Dreams . . . dreams
fill life with guidance
to grab the chances of one's soul . . .
and soar into the sunset.

Waves sleep
on a sandy beach,
somewhere in a place
where shells of silver live.

Shadow: Concrete and Champagne
Muse: DeLeon, Singer

"When"
<u>In the House</u>

Black curls and leather hats,
silver earrings and eyes that sparkle
like champagne . . .

features an artist
singing in a
world of concrete . . .

chipping away at that which covers
the heartbeat that must break
barriers . . .

to feel the love of
the one with black curls
and necklaces.

Shadow: Bubbling Adrenaline
Muse: Robin Williams, Actor

Features of spontaneity
live on your adorable face.
Expressions of amusement radiate from your eyes
while smiling cheeks laugh.

Your lips dance to the speed
of your adrenaline
trying to keep pace
with your thoughts.

You adorn my life with gifts of happiness;
the awesome talent breeding within your soul
fascinates my eye's hunger
for scenes of your presence.

You know boundaries don't exist,
and you are fearless of the reactions
which bubble up inside of you . . .
surviving perfectly within the present moment.

You're an adorable man possessing a spirit of adventure,
growing an abundance of love, humor, and excitement
for your artistry . . .
possessing a deep affection for humor.

Shadow: Passionate Portrayal
Muse: John Travolta, Actor

*George Malley
is another character to portray
the simple life in small town existence.
A surgeon of metal and motors,
a background filled with noises, tools;
grease covering the cement floor.*

*A man's passion
is sometimes content,
sometimes struggling with patience,
but always aware
of the opportunities
that allow that passion to live.*

*George Malley
a character who portrays the actor,
a caring man with a kind passion.
Some people don't possess this intensity,
some never can,
others won't.*

*The mechanic in a small town is content
as he lives his dream as an actor,
smiling,
realizing that
his passion
is free.*

Shadow: Gold Vibrations
Muse: Fugees, Musicians / Band

Lauryn, Pras, Clef
a family of three.
Taking "The Score"
from city to city.

Humble, talented
caring, and true. . .
The pop music world
gained something remarkably new!

The "have-nots" are central
negativity forever banned
creating beauty with vibes
taking a stand.

In the universe of music
lives Haitian-American rap,
music vibrating coast to coast
traveling the map.

"Killing Me Softly"
lingers, a song to behold.
Instruments accompany
beautiful voices of gold. . .

Shadow: Life Is But a Dream
Muse: Jim Carrey, Actor

When I think of you,
a smile appears in my thoughts
because you make me laugh!

The characters you produce
appear to bulge from
your inability to maintain control.

Life is but a dream
as you row yourself into worlds unknown
merrily, merrily down a stream

approaching the present,
you awaken to the sounds of reality
realizing that life can be
a dream come true!

Shadow: Visual Discipline
Muse: Arnold Schwarzenegger, Actor

*Massive muscles live
on a disciplined physique
displaying a sense of a strong, bold
and fearless exterior.*

*Movies finished, watched and critiqued;
some funny . . .
but most taking audiences
over the edge of excitement.*

*There appeared a helicopter scene;
a terrorizing thrill of its flying through a tunnel
. . . knowing the risks . . .
proceeding anyway.*

*Visual effects have married your characters
allowing the successes
of ultimate action adventures
and hilarious films
displaying a man who is confident,
strong, and disciplined.*

Shadow: Humanity
Muse: Sylvester Stallone, Actor

Maybe I wanted to learn about Vietnam
or perhaps just journey with you
in a world I'd never prepared for . . . nor would I ever survive in
a jungle of disease,
both in nature and in man.

Your character, Rambo, gives me courage
and I feel safe
because your character possesses
that which is necessary
to kill . . . the disease.

You sought the existence of
men who were shackled to themselves
breaking their resistance,
forcing them to survive
in a cage of inhumanity, the brutality of the disease.

Your determination to save any scraps
of dignity left within their souls . . . was powerful.
There was nothing that could deter
you from freeing these men
left to rot in a jungle . . . so far from home.

You understood, felt their pain
a prisoner of manipulation yourself once,
you witnessed the disease . . .
a pain
that still haunts many men.

Pursuing a mission manifested within your soul,
you freed them, giving back that which
was stolen from them,
enabling me to believe in
your devotion . . . to humanity.

Shadow: Mountain Perfume
Muse: Tina Turner, Singer

A mountain view,
Lilies of the Valley growing below,
listening to your voice
watching you sit calmly on the mountain's edge.

A cool breeze is aroused
as gentle echoes of your soul penetrate nature.
You reach within your solitude for words of beauty,
. . . of experience.

A beautiful gift of sound
embraces the mountains,
and they admire the musical notes,
vocal and strong . . .

that linger in their presence, floating in the sunlight
down to the valley below
sprinkling the lilies with drops
of scented sounds created by your soul.

Shadow: Highway 1
Muse: Teri Garr, Actress

I don't know the "time," don't want to.
Life, to me . . . isn't measured, just visited.
I tag along with you on a casual, free ride.
The breeze tangos with my hair
as we cruise down Highway 1 in your convertible.

A surfer describes his hobby
as "dancing with the waves."
Those words dive into my soul
while my imagination surfs the ocean.

Watching the "rain forest" people as they live their days
made me realize that I could not survive there.
I crave the sun, dunes, and each grain of beach life.
The rain is cleansing, but I who would measure "time," don't want to.

Eating a raw oyster
proved you are courageous,
perhaps just adventurous!
I decline, don't want to measure "time."

A photographer on the shore
catches "time" in squares,
preserving the moments passed,
taking them into the future. . .

The adorable bookstore in town is my favorite,
having saved a lot of "time" in search of
discoveries that I will find
living among the shelves . . .

A chainsaw sculptor, how very unique.
He claims that he makes "sawdust."
. . . perhaps the sawdust are pieces of "time"
spent creating wooden masterpieces.

Thank you, Teri, for your "time" spent
sharing the wonder and treasures found
on Highway 1.

Shadow: Flames of Nostalgia
Muse: Cher, Singer / Actress

Nostalgic . . . yet in tune with today . . .
your aura is warm, like candle flames
burning silver reflections of your immense presence.

Rays of strength outline your beauty
your eyes, tender . . . and powerful
capture the experiences of your life.

A sculptor's dream, a photographer's wish
you radiate an inner peace like
the scent of musk oil flowing from an incense coil.

The peacefulness and uniqueness of your soul
has to be a sanctuary
for the talents and abilities that you possess.

The flames of nostalgia burn forever
within my admiration
for your talented, courageous and beautiful aura.

Shadow: Gifts
Muse: Tom Hanks, Actor

Deep behind your smiling eyes
lives fun and adventure,
a playful land of tremendous wonder.

You've exposed a variety of personalities,
bringing stories to life.
The magnitude of your talents is a force truly appreciated
and evident through many memorable movies.

The diversity of the characters that you portray
gives audiences outrageous gifts of laughter
and some
make us contemplate life.

The driving forces behind
your deep eyes . . . smile,
revealing the immense talent
that surrounds your creative artistry.

Shadow: Release
Muse: Bruce Willis, Actor

Courageous, humorous, a fun-loving guy
possessing an inner confidence
in life, in movies . . .

Tough, rugged, a man of strength
able to maneuver danger
with a smile.

Intelligent, clever, a skillful marksman,
knowledgeable about weapons . . .
beating the odds.

Lovable, cuddly, handsome too,
a fun-loving guy
exposed in life, in movies,

allowing audiences to release stressful emotions
through your daring, adventurous characters

and perhaps, realize that you
are an ordinary guy
with extraordinary talent.

Shadow: Internal Affairs
Muse: Brenda Vaccaro, Actress
Touched by an Angel

An angel flew through heaven's airwaves,
an expert sent on a mission
to perform crisis intervention.
A message deserving of your ability
to deliver its direct simplicity and powerful impact.

"Messing up God's plan!"
Ridiculous, His plan is
impossible to tamper with.
No one, not even His angels, possess omniscience.
. . . A powerful message, a reminder too . . .

of a power that places us
where His plan requires us to be . . .
to pass through the lives of those
He knows need the human qualities
that each of us "do" possess.

Each of us are to learn
from those He puts us in contact with
to ensure every piece of His plan fits together
like a puzzle.

You are the "master"
of playing inspirational roles
that require a powerful energy,
a graceful humor,
and tremendous honesty.

Shadow: A Gentle Guide
Muse: John Dye, Actor
Touched by an Angel

*Your character is
the most gentle, understanding
and loving portrayal of humanity.*

*Traits required for one who must lead lives,
assisting them in their transition
from earth into heaven . . .*

*to begin their lives as a spirit,
which is really the substance they always were
deep within.*

*Some hide in their physical forms,
some are able to escape the physical forms,
and some realize for the first time that God is waiting . . .*

*in a place for each of His children,
as you guide them into the light
and take them home.*

Shadow: Aura in a Ford Bronco
Muse: George Clooney, Actor

The ultimate journey into existence . . .
that place, no hassles,
the passage leading to perspective
to escape that which becomes overwhelming . . .

to seek freedom within seclusion
to sort facts which demand
explanations from the mind,
the conscious element of thoughts.

When analyzing the reality of success,
the mind questions the soul,
the origin of the natural order of life,
the immortal essence within.

The soul coordinates with the heart,
the pulse of emotions
so that the natural order of life within
is in complete harmony . . .

ensuring that the journey
into existence
evolves into the acceptance
of reality.

Shadow: Stillness
Muse: Patty Duke, Actress

I don't have to see you to know
your image is on the TV.
Your voice lingers around me
and I am drawn into room where you are . . .
to watch in awe, another character
that you portray.

The imagination and energy
that you possess was always present . . . somehow.
Your eyes reflect a stillness
that is never still,
for all the passages within
your journey were not all visible.

You are an inspirational actress,
your beauty endless, your voice pure,
your talent amazing,
and I am honored
each time I can be
in the same room with you.

Shadow: Priceless
Muse: Bonnie Bedelia, Actress

Your voice is a unique song,
a sensual tune, soft yet powerful,
spoken with care . . . illuminating your eyes.

Mrs. McClain . . .
was a priceless portrayal
of values that are important.

At the same time,
many audiences who watched you punch and shock
that overbearing, rude reporter . . . were satisfied!

You are a beautiful woman
possessing a warm softness which
embraces feminity entwined with strength.

Shadow: Magical Memories
Muse: Sammy Davis, Jr., Entertainer

Fearing an audience
did not exist within you,
passion overflowed from your heart . . .

tapping into lives of many people
creating magical memories,
dancing under a universe of gold.

Stages you touched
were honored with your presence,
audiences in awe of your talent . . .

captured by the
genuine love in your eyes and
the brilliant smile you freely shared.

Shadow: Protection
Muse: Gene Hackman, Actor

If I were in your movies, I would follow
you anywhere, trusting you completely.

The roles you portray are remarkably intelligent
and extremely persuasive.

Your art is vibrantly alive
when danger lurks in scene after scene.

Fear doesn't seem to know you
during confrontations with possible death.

You maintain control
and continue towards the mission,

leading characters to safety,
rescuing someone, or fighting for what is "right."

You are a distinguished and handsome man
with roles requiring your passion and spirit.

P.S. I would have followed you through the Poseidon.

Shadow: Simmering Smile
Muse: Danny Glover, Actor

A smile brightens those natural traits
of an actor who has what it takes
to win the hearts of all who watch films reflecting
sincerity and warmth.

You are likable, lovable, handsome
and comical, sharing the laughter
of your personality while
smiling intensely.

These natural attributes of those
characters you portray
must be as vital as when you
are not acting.

Your presence on screen erupts with a talent
which I believe always simmered within your heart
exploding when the time appeared for you
to soar into a future unknown.

Shadow: Music of the Spheres
Muse: Yanni, Musician

*. . . masterpieces in the past
impact musical artistry of today
as instruments become alive
from the touch of those who admire the potential
that lies in each one . . .*

*Musicians gather in the ruins
of times long ago,
creating and merging sounds that
touch the spirits
that once walked the land of Greece.*

*Pythagoras feels the tremors of your talent,
smiling with appreciation
for your ability to arrange vibrations,
composing rhythms that resemble the beauty
of the "music of the spheres."*

*The spirit world is touched
by your presence, entranced by your
immense talent
to bring to them the sound
of times long ago.*

Shadow: Feathers in the Wind
Muse: Stefanie Powers, Actress

. . . Feathers in the wind . . . and
Sunrises of pink and lavender surround
your being, an angel of the world,

flying to lands unknown
capturing the essence of freedom
with sunsets of crimson and gold,

touching the lives of those you encounter
leaving impressions of love.
A departure in the wind

leads you to Kenya,
the gentle, stupendous landscape
filled with animals of the wild.

A sunray touches earth,
. . . your elegance sparkles
like a diamond, pure and radiant.

A woman whose generosity
to the wild, supporting their needs
is admirable . . . loving, and kind,

and free, like feathers in the wind.

Shadow: Magnetic
Muse: Angela Bassett, Actress

Serene and gentle,
a beautymark on the screen,
enriching plots.

Taking a road
into the excitement of film
leaving imprints of pearls.

You are magnetic,
pulling audiences into an adventure
to follow you into depths unknown.

Serene and gentle,
you shine like a star
illuminating hearts of those close . . . and far.

Shadow: Treasured Feeling
Muse: Eddie Murphy, Actor

Treasures are abundant . . .
as are your talents.
Characters are creatively born
from your artistry of humor.

Awesome performances
reveal your incredible talent and skill,
an illuminating energy that is never still . . .

Taking chances, running wild,
laughing and smiling
waiting . . . knowing it's there, somewhere.

That treasured feeling that
encompasses the abundance
of pathways waiting just for you.

Shadow: Calm and Confident
Muse: Steven Seagal, Actor

Tall, handsome,
a rough exterior . . . dressed in black.
Hands of steel,
a mind of meditation touches my thoughts;
thought tremors I can feel
when I watch your performances.

Your martial artistry is fast and quick,
possessing the ultimate confidence
found within your characters,
. . . never worried, never scared,
intelligent, humorous,
and intensely gorgeous.

Somewhere within the characters
of martial artistry,
I believe that you are a man who reaches
places within your mind
that are comfortable . . . relaxing in a state that is
unobtainable to many.

Your eyes fill with knowledge
of an ancient instruction that enriches
your soul, calming your heartbeat
as you meditate within scents and sounds
that are authentically your possessions . . .
and revealed within your artistry.

Shadow: Bronze Sunrise
Muse: Bruce Hornsby, Musician

. . . like a sunrise . . .
your smile peeks over the ocean horizon.
It seems far away.

Hearing your voice,
the sea waves.

Reflections of your words
float calmly
and shine brightly.

Words flow from your soul
as your eyes of passion close.

Natural tan facial features . . .
expressive, like a bronze mythology god,
touch my soul.

Your fingers dance upon the piano keyboard
creating intensity . . .

A man who easily creates feelings of freedom
that take me sailing in a sea
that seems far away . . .

Shadow: Illumination
Muse: Elizabeth Taylor, Actress

*Your voice is gentle possessing
a natural sensuality and kindness.
A queen among actresses, your
loving spirit touches many people.*

*A tender soul living within a world of harshness
is extremely sensitive to the
needs of people
who are suffering everywhere.*

*Dedication isn't a strong enough word
for the humanity expressed
from your deep and spiritual
support of AIDS.*

*You have given your heartfelt
love to a world in need of your
unending belief and courage,
caring for human beings.*

*Love has to be your favorite
and most nurtured feeling.
In a world of turmoil, you sparkle
like a white diamond, illuminating hope.*

Shadow: Ignition
Muse: Tom Cruise, Actor, for his love of flying

Feeling the sensuality of your own heart beat
flames of anticipation pump quickly in the midst of a desert heat.
An internal rush of passionate adrenaline flows
and in your eyes, a vibrance of mischief glows.
All the earth's elements feel so right,
in the depths of your soul, a fire ignites,
allowing you to indulge yourself in the pleasures of adventure.
Raw thoughts of skill spark intense feelings so pure.
You breathe deeply soaring far into the sky of white and gray
where the clouds become your companions as you fly away
into the universe...that's where you want to be
intoxicated by the earth's elements, realizing the intensity
of the explosion within your heart, you find
that cruising the altitudes totally frees the mind
of the thoughts and feelings left down below
climbing the atmosphere, it's what you know
of life, love, and happiness, your free ambition
is sustained forever within the sound of ignition.

Shadow: Another Realm
Muses: Roberta Flack and Luther Vandross, Singers

poetic
two souls melting into
sensual sounds of love and admiration
carrying creativity
into another realm

a powerful display of unique gifts
explosive...tender
joining forces to become a duet
carrying creativity
into another realm

handsome and beautiful
Luther and Roberta
an enchanting brilliance shines
as you carry creativity
into another realm

Shadow: Exultation
Muse: Whitney Houston, Singer / Actress

*a celebration of songs
nurturing the music of gospel
is instrumental in teaching
those feelings of exultation
that give us strength
to grasp the opportunities
that can lead to victory.*

*You continue to nourish souls
through the genuine vibrations of your heart
sharing the birthright of your voice
giving many a keepsake to be treasured
forever, savored over the years
that shall continue to touch upon love
hope, happiness...and freedom.*

*A glistening, silvery charm
dangling from the bluest sky
filling our souls with that gift
of elegance you share singing gospel
which represents a beautiful sachet
that we place in our hearts
to radiate the sounds that exult us...*

Shadow: Time Waves
Muse: Madonna, Singer / Actress

Surfing the unknown waves of time
following the inevitable flow
of each evolving second
in which love will grow.

One smile of your beauty
tenderly touches the sunshine,
experiencing the happiness
of your life in its prime.

A tender, young child
cuddled in your arms at night
listening to the lullabyes
staring at your eyes shining bright.

Indulging in the depths
of an ocean's peace
brings you quiet moments
through the barrier reefs
of another world

where you are comfortable
restful as a dream at day
where time is not allowed
to exist in any other way.

Shadow: Emerald Images
Muse: Garth Brooks, C&W Singer

Running free in the emerald fields of your being,
seeing the images of illuminating strength.
Your entrance into their world leaves you breathless
as you wander through a pleasurable atmosphere
sensing the vitality that surrounds your being.
You realize the privilege of visiting those exciting moments
which have waited for you to discover the emerald field
of endless peace that defines you...your songs.
Images of your soul are happy now
bearing gifts of fresh horses...
awaiting your next visit.

P.S.
The black and white billboard caught my eye, the words "sold-out"
glared as I drove by,
appearing at the Hampton Coliseum, the one and only Garth Brooks,
possessing a voice of country thoughts...and handsome cowboy looks.
Saw you last night on TV, winning the "People's Choice Award," and
for your acceptance speech
I thank the Lord, telling us that 1997 would be the best yet for our
careers and goals...
your inspiration, I'll never forget...

Shadow: Channel of Compassion
Muse: Hillary Rodham Clinton

*three words...form one entity
the first lady...
a title you deserve*

*the intensity in which you perform
your duties is overwhelming...
the strength and commitment of your heart
are apparent in every speech, interview...
you are forthright, serious...through compassion*

*and you believe in your destiny
to make a difference within the United States
to fulfill the needs of all people
to make available all benefits which the people
deserve...*

*to enhance lives
and promote unity
through continuous hard work
which I know comes easy to you...
because you possess the serenity of your soul
and have become one with nature
to realize what pure potential is...
and you live it every day.*

*Thank you for realizing
how your abilities and skills are an important
part of a greater plan...*

Shadow: Alone with Leon
Muse: Leon Russell, Musician / Singer

...cruising Virginia's interstate
every morning, every night,
during golden sunrises
into the midst of evening light.
Hearing the passionate reflection
as only the legendary Leon knows it,
listening to the surging words
of a mellow musical poet.
He's desirably easy to be with
allowing me to experience many things...
contemplating the ideas of his thoughts
when his inhibitions escape as he sings.
We walk upon an invisible tight wire
in the midst of a darkness known,
masquerading as meditating spirits
together in our journey, sometimes alone.
Viewing the structural world around us
knowing...and accepting that we may not belong
to the concrete constraints of man
allowing us to become transcendent within a song...

Shadow: Sicilian Sweetheart
Muse: Loretta LaRoche, Medical Humorist, about her video, "Joy of Stress"

The loudest, wildest laughter filled a room of people,
you know, those who are constantly stressed!
We absolutely enjoyed your methods of stressing the importance
of humor in all our daily lives!

You are a sweetheart, an Italian meatball in spaghetti sauce
the main spicy Sicilian part of our society!

Teaching us the freedom to giggle, the beginning of a hearty laugh.
I wonder how many of us really wonder about the humor
in each stressful situation?

We can stop and meditate about the situation we find ourselves in
and know that it really isn't worth our time
to take it too seriously, so let's all begin to stop
and listen to our funny bones
sharing the laughter within our souls
(releasing the inner joy of knowing)
that laughter is healthier as we continue to grow
in the midst of our society
let's all kiss stress good-bye!

Exploration

An exciting, fun and powerful exploration into your world
led me to an inner quest to touch your lives
as you have touched mine.
Until the next journey,

"the moon is the shadow of our minds,
the stars are shadows of our dreams,
the planets are shadows of our creativity
the clouds are shadows of our spirits
and the raindrops rinse our souls . . .
so we can be a shadow of God"
Angie

Muses in My Music Box

. . . earth and heaven are filled with shadows
that supply the soul with inspiration . . .

I hope that the treasures
found within this first volume of the shadows
of my muses will be discovered
and cherished . . . by many.

the sounds in my music box
are continuously playing, as more shadows emerge . . .

Just a few of Volume II Shadows . . .
Tim Allen
Kurt Russell
Brett Butler
Denzel Washington
Reba McEntire
Kelsey Grammar
Jamie Lee Curtis
Donna Summer
Will Smith

Postscript

I've heard various comments about poetry; the most popular being, "I don't understand poetry." For that reason, works of poetry have not been a part of many people's lives. People relate Shakespeare to poetry, having dreaded this subject during their education. That was then . . . this is now . . . . I want to reveal poems that are easy to relate to, that are fun to read, and that are written with understandable words.

I have read poems written from the beautiful hearts of children, the admirable writings of many adults, and poems written from the intense perspectives of teenagers. At poetry readings, I have listened to teenagers read poems in which they search for love, explain broken relationships, try to understand why they are unloved, and what they did wrong. My heart fills with compassion for our teenagers, and I want them to know that they are loved and that relationships formed so early in life are temporary learning experiences, steppingstones toward adulthood.

Poetry is extremely important to poets of all ages, of all cultures and of all races. I hope all of us feel compelled to raise the awareness of today's poetry and celebrate the works of our poets around the world. Someday I hope to work for the Rosie O'Donnell Show *and be given that unique assignment to seek out poets around the world, to share with audiences the beauty and variety of poetry created by men, women, and our sweet children. If a career with the* Rosie O'Donnell Show *is part of God's plan for me, it will manifest. If not, I know God has another plan for me that I will accept proudly because I know it's the only pathway for my life's journey.*

This volume is the first in a twelve-volume series about famous people who have inspired me. I know many more people will inspire me in the future. I hope this is the beginning of a long relationship with you. I invite you to experience the world of poetry and hope you can find enjoyment, fun, and understanding within the artistry of poetry.